OLIVER
TRACTORS

Sherry Schaefer
and Jeff Hackett

OLIVER OC-156 DIESEL

OLIVER

Voyageur Press

This edition published in 2001 by Voyageur Press, an imprint of MBI Publishing Company, Galtier Plaza, Suite 200, 380 Jackson Street, St. Paul, MN 55101 USA

MBI Publishing Company titles are also available at discounts in bulk quantity for industrial or sales-promotional use. For details write to Special Sales Manager at MBI Publishing Company, Galtier Plaza, Suite 200, 380 Jackson Street, St. Paul, MN 55101 USA.

Library of Congress Cataloging-in-Publication Data Available

ISBN-13: 978-0-7603-0736-6
ISBN 0-7603-0736-9

On the front cover: The Supers were merely updated versions of the former Fleetline series. Nearly all of the parts were interchangeable, but the main difference was the bore and stroke of the engine. This line was produced in a wide variety of configurations and made it a model that could be fit to a farmer's particular needs. When the Supers were originally introduced, they had green wheels, but the buyers expressed their favoritism to the red wheels, and Oliver changed the color back to red in 1957.

On the frontispiece: The tiptoe steel wheels were patented by the Oliver Chilled Plow Works while they were designing their first tractor. This design was carried over to the newly formed Oliver Farm Equipment Company and was a great success. These wheels enabled the tractor to operate with little soil compaction or risk of getting stuck.

On the title page: Highway yellow became the standard color for the crawler line after 1951. The OC-3 was the smallest crawler produced at that time, and although the OC-18 was the largest, the OC-156 was the largest machine with a loader. Both machines were powered by Hercules engines, but the OC-3 had only 22 horsepower versus the OC-15's nearly 95 horses.

On the contents page: The 30-60 was undoubtedly the most popular, large Hart-Parr tractor built. Its dependability earned it the name "Old Reliable." Nearly 4,000 of these machines were built, and many of them were exported worldwide. Most of these workhorses were scrapped when they were replaced by the smaller cross-motor tractors. This particular unit (serial number 4926) resides at the Floyd County Museum in Charles City, Iowa; the birthplace of the tractor industry.

On the back cover: "IT'S BETTER TO BUY AN OLIVER THAN TO WISH YOU HAD." This is how Oliver promoted their popular 70. When this tractor first arrived at the dealerships, it was kept under a sheet until it was unveiled to the public on October 15, 1937. The 70 was also the first model in the Oliver family to have six cylinders.

Edited by Amy Glaser
Designed by LeAnn Kuhlmann

Printed in China

CONTENTS

Chapter One

Founders of the Tractor Industry

In the late 1800s steam power was the most commonly used source of horsepower for the farmer. But the Industrial Revolution was rapidly changing industry, and agriculture would be a forerunner in this new age of mechanization.

The 20-40 was the largest tricycle-styled tractor built by Hart-Parr. Production of this model ran from 1911-1914. The only known restored model is at home in Charles City, Iowa, where it all began.

The Little Devil was Hart and Parr's failed attempt to produce a successful small tractor. A premium trade-in price was offered to farmers who had acquired one of the machines. Hart-Parr then destroyed the tractors, making them very hard to locate today. *Floyd County Historical Society*

The three-wheeled design of the Little Devil made the tractor unstable when turning or on rough ground. A guard was added under the seat to protect the operator and prevent the tractor from tipping too far. *Floyd County Historical Society*

Two young engineering students had big plans for their future and for a new source of power that would revolutionize the farming industry: Charles Hart, of Charles City, Iowa, and Charles Parr, a Wyoming, Wisconsin native. Hart and Parr met in 1894 at the University of Wisconsin, found they were both fascinated by the early developments in internal combustion engines, and began to work together to design and build their own stationary gasoline engines.

By 1897 they had formed the Hart-Parr Company in Madison, Wisconsin. Their engines were so successful that within three years they had outgrown their factory. However, the city of Madison had no desire to become an industrial area, leaving little possibility of expansion for Hart-Parr. Charles City, Iowa, was more than willing to welcome them to their city, and in 1901 the young entrepreneurs moved back to Hart's hometown.

It was at this factory that they decided to use their engines to power the first successful, commercially produced tractor. Hart-Parr No. 1 was built in 1902 and was sold to an Iowa farmer who used it for several years. The delivery of this tractor was a big event and every significant person at the Hart-Parr works went along to witness this monumental milestone. It should have been a simple trip but as dozens of witnesses watched, the heavy tractor broke through a wooden bridge and landed in a creek bottom. The machine did not receive any major damage, and it was retrieved with a team of horses. This was the beginning of what would become a long line of successes for the Hart-Parr Company.

Hart and Parr knew they were on the right track with their machine. There were disadvantages using horses for power on the farm. Horses had to be tended year-round. There were daily chores, shoeing, and the expense of feed. On average, every horse required 5 acres for feed: on a 50-acre farm, 20 percent was consumed by a two-horse team.

There were also many disadvantages using steam power. Large quantities of fuel and water continuously taken to the field proved to be rather expensive, and many lives were lost because of boiler explosions. Like it or not, steam power was on its way out. One would think that farmers using steam would be looking for an alternative source of power, but this was not necessarily the case. Steam was still a great improvement over horses, and farmers were reluctant to switch to a new form of power that they knew nothing about. Hart-Parr's gas engine tractor was met with much opposition, especially by the steam engine manufacturers. Many of the companies that had supported *The American Thresherman,* a magazine dedicated to farmers, threatened to withdraw all of their advertising if the magazine continued to let Hart-Parr advertise.

As was typical during the Industrial Revolution, new machines and new ideas were viewed with much skepticism. Nothing with a combustion engine had ever been used before, and ignorance turned to fear. If complications with the machine arose in the field, there was no one qualified to fix it. Yet, the tractor proved to be so successful that farmers started to take notice, and by 1902 a run of 13 model 17-30 tractors were in production at Hart-Parr.

The fourth tractor in this production run is well-known among collectors. Originally sold to George Mitchell, it was bought back by Hart-Parr for advertising purposes and toured at many fairs and tractor events as the oldest gasoline tractor in existence. From 1932 to 1948 this tractor, known as "Old Hart-Parr No. 3," was on display at the Museum of Science and Industry in Chicago. It later became part of the Smithsonian collection where it has been displayed there and at other museums.

The following model, the 22-40, was built from 1903–1911. Because of compression ratio changes, the rating on this tractor was changed to

Power units such as the one used on this air compressor were very successful for the company. Its engines earned the reputation of being reliable and having long lives.

22-45 during 1908. This unit was originally designed to burn gasoline, but gasoline was becoming less available and more costly, so Hart-Parr set out to find an alternative. After rigorous testing, the two young inventors perfected the first known method of burning kerosene for fuel. They equipped all their engines with the new Hart-Parr system and immediately cut fuel costs in half. The savings during that first quarter of the century ran into millions. In 1906 there were approximately 600 tractors being used in the United States; of those, one-third of them were Hart-Parrs.

Subsequent models of tractors produced by other companies used an adaptation of the original Hart-Parr method that was never patented. By 1928, 75 percent of all tractors built were operating on kerosene—Hart-Parr's gift to the industry. The partners were never too concerned about patenting any of their numerous inventions, they were more focused on putting them right to work in their products.

The model 30-60, produced from 1911 to 1916, was so dependable that it was nicknamed "Old Reliable." This model was basically the

The dependability of the 30-60 earned this model the name of "Old Reliable." It was sold in large quantities worldwide for farm and industrial use. *Floyd County Historical Society*

same as the 22-45. But because of breakage on previous models, the axle size was increased from 4 to 5 inches. This was probably the most successful of the big machines produced by the company and production numbers were in the thousands. Unfortunately, the majority of these machines were melted down for scrap-iron drives during the war.

The two most mysterious models in the line have to be the 40-80 and the 60-100. It is believed that there were only 10 40-80 horsepower units built. It was first exhibited at the Minnesota State Fair in 1908. The tractor weighed 34,000 pounds and was so big that it didn't interest many farmers—an operator would have to use a ladder just to get on the tractor. It did not produce the results that Hart-Parr was expecting. The 40-80 used a different design from previous models. It had a

four-cylinder engine that used a separate radiator for each set of cylinders, the radiators were mounted on the rear of the frame, and the front end had closely spaced wheels. At present, none of these tractors have been located.

By far, the most elusive model is the 60-100. This monstrous machine weighed in at over 50,000 pounds. It is not known if more than one was built; it was considered an experimental unit and never went into production. Some think that Hart-Parr was working with Russia to build them powerful machines for use in their quarries.

Hart-Parr had proved its success with reliable tractors, but farmers were asking for a machine with better maneuverability. With this in mind, the company introduced the 15-30. The 15-30 was a tricycle-type machine that was capable of turning much sharper than the wide-front

The Moto-Meter was the forerunner to a temperature gauge. These were used on Hart-Parr's cross-motor tractors until gauges became regular equipment. *Bill Campbell*

The winged-radiator cap was easily recognized as Hart-Parr's trademark logo. This cap was used on the cross-motor tractor in place of the Moto-Meter. *Bill Campbell*

The Oil King was a popular tractor for roadwork. This crew of township officers is undoubtedly comparing their new tractor's ability to that of the team of horses which it replaced. *Sherry Schaefer collection*

units of the past. This tractor was even equipped with a road gear capable of the "frightening" speed of 4 miles per hour.

In 1911, the 15-30 was upgraded to a 20-40. It used the same basic engine and design of its little brother with only minor changes. The front wheel was smaller but twice as wide to support the weight of the front end. There is currently only one 20-40 known and it is owned by the Floyd County Historical Society in Charles City, Iowa.

The next tractor to be built was a smaller unit, a 12-27. It used a single-cylinder vertical engine designed to burn kerosene. The tricycle configuration was similar to that used in previous models except it employed two small narrow wheels in front instead of one wide one. The exhaust was located behind the engine and hampered the operator's view. After building 224 of these machines, the engine was upgraded and the tractor became an 18-35. Weighing in at around 11,000 pounds, it was not as heavy as other tractors but was capable of producing more power. There were around 250 of these units produced until 1919, but by then, the tricycle design proved to be unstable

and the idea was abandoned by nearly all tractor manufacturers.

By the mid-1910s the trend was moving away from the bigger machines. The Corn Belt farmers wanted a smaller version that was easier to maneuver and was more affordable. Charles Hart had just attended the 1914 tractor trials in Fremont, Nebraska, and was excited about the design of the small Bull tractor. He quickly set out to build a small tractor of his own. The result was a strange-looking three-wheeled machine called the Little Devil. Rated as a 15-22, the 6,600-pound machine had a wide front axle and a single drive wheel in the rear. The tractor was rushed into production prior to testing and resulted in a recall of all machines. To reverse the tractor, the operator would idle the engine down, kill the spark, and kick the engine backwards to reverse the direction that the motor rotated. This might have been a good idea except the tractor would often jump into reverse when the engine was idled down, causing many deaths. Another defective feature was the machine's inability to balance itself, causing the tractor to tip toward the right. Production of the Little Devil ceased in 1916.

The 1920s were economically draining for Hart-Parr. Tractor production dropped from 203,207 tractors in 1920 to 73,198 tractors in 1921. Business income dropped from $6 million a year to $600,000 in 1924. Even so, more farms were converting to "tractor farms" and the leaders of the company held on to their faith that power farming was the future. On January 1, 1920, there were 246,083 tractors on American farms. By January 1, 1925, the number had escalated to 506,745.

During the early 1920s, Hart-Parr engineers were busy perfecting a completely new tractor design. This new lighter tractor, known as the 12-25, was the basis from which the rest of the tractor line was developed. This machine had a horizontal, two-cylinder, heavy-duty, slow-speed engine that was lubricated with fresh, force-fed oil. After testing in Nebraska, the tractor was re-rated as a 15-30, to be known merely as the "30." In 1924 it was replaced with the 16-30, only to be upgraded again in 1926 to an 18-36.

It was during the period from 1917 to 1921 that the fame of the 30 extended the market to every state and many foreign countries. It also was during this time that Charles Hart sold his interest in the company back to his original backers and moved to Montana.

Some companies opted to follow the designs of the Hart-Parr engine while others tried to adapt the same upright four-cylinder styling used by the automotive industry. However, Hart-Parr continued to show its supremacy for power, low cost of operation, and long life. In competitive fuel demonstrations, they were constantly at the top.

In 1920, a smaller version of the 30 was introduced. The 10-20, or "20," was classified as a two-plow tractor with a two-cylinder horizontal engine. Production of this tractor continued until 1924 when it was replaced by the 12-24.

Introduced in 1923, the 22-40 was nearly 2,000 pounds heavier than the 30. The four-cylinder engine was basically two 10-20 engines with 616 inches of displacement. This tractor was promoted heavily for road building and maintenance jobs. It remained on the market until 1927 when it was replaced by the 28-50. This twin-engine unit was powered with two 12-24 blocks. In 1928 this tractor listed for $2,085; a $75 deduction was made if it was ordered without a cab.

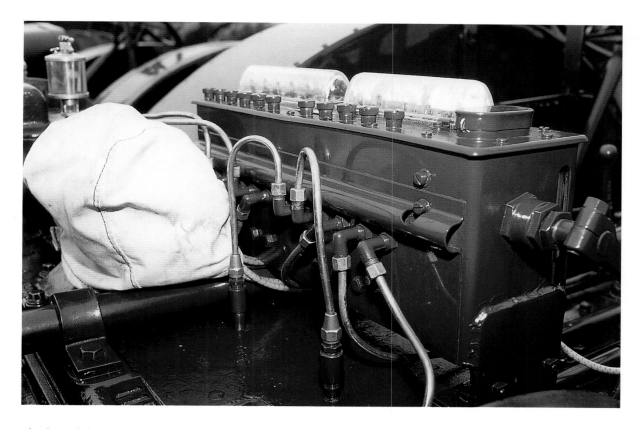

The force-fed oil lubrication system was one of Hart-Parr's many innovations. This method was much more efficient than the older "drip" lubrication, which failed if neglected.

The 28-50 also was available in an industrial version with solid rubber tires. This was the last Hart-Parr model introduced; the company would soon merge with an implement manufacturer to become a full-line agricultural-machinery supplier.

The word "tractor" was first used by Hart-Parr in a June 1907 advertisement put together by sales manager W. H. Williams, who wanted to shorten the lengthy phrase "gasoline traction engine." The new word caught on and was subsequently used by other manufacturers. The word "tractor" had been used prior to that time in an 1870 patent, but Hart-Parr is credited with making the word part of the English language.

Hart-Parr had succeeded in revolutionizing the farming industry. Its many innovations changed the way of engine and machinery building and farming for many throughout the world. They developed the first oil-cooled engine: Oil was advantageous to water because it would not freeze in cold weather. The system pumped hot oil from the engine through the radiator where a vacuum created from the exhaust would pull air through the fins. The air would cool the circulating oil with every breath the big machine took, and the oil would be pumped back to the crankcase where the sequence was repeated.

Charlie Parr, one of the "Founders of the Tractor Industry," proudly stands beside the early Hart-Parr, rated a 17-30, and the new 18-28. Twenty-six years had passed between the production of each of the two models. While the horsepower was nearly the same, the size had decreased considerably. *Sherry Schaefer collection*

The reliable Hart-Parrs were used for more than farming as demonstrated by this 22-45. Moving large boilers across Texas was still a chore, but less work for all with a Hart-Parr. *Sherry Schaefer collection*

Force-fed lubrication was also developed by Hart-Parr. This system proved to be much more adequate than drip lubrication and helped eliminate some of the costly repairs due to neglect. The company's valve-in-head engine was much more efficient than the L-head engines that had valves in the crankcase. The valve-in-head engine was more economical and easier to maintain.

Among its modern innovations was the multiple-speed transmission. This allowed the machine more versatility so farmers could accomplish chores previously done by horses. Also, the transmission and final-drive gears were built heavy-duty, adding to its longevity and reliability.

In 1926 they once again slashed fuel costs in half for the farmer by perfecting the burning of low-grade fuels such as distillate and furnace oils in their tractors. Hart-Parr was the first to stake their reputation on their fuel system and ordered their tractors officially tested on distillate at the Nebraska tests. This created quite a stir among other tractor manufacturers.

Hart-Parr recognized that they were getting some competition by others jumping into the industry that they had founded. They began to look beyond the U.S. borders for sales prospects. Trade contracts were set up with sales agents in Buenos Aires, Argentina, and Austria. Tractors also were shipped into Cuba, Chile, and the Philippine Islands. These markets proved to be very successful and expansions were made into Russia, Africa, and Europe, making Hart-Parr known world-wide.

Chapter Two

Oliver Enters the Tractor Market

The year 1929 brought about many changes for the Oliver Chilled Plow Works, in South Bend, Indiana. The benefits of power farming were obvious and the trend was growing towards this new way of farming.

The High Compression Special was an upgraded version of the 28-44 that was designed to burn the newer high-octane fuels. It was eventually replaced by the four-cylinder 99. *Dennis Baker*

You didn't have to bed down a tractor or feed it all winter, the tractor didn't need to rest at the end of the furrow, and it covered a lot more land by the end of the day. Oliver had the foresight to see this and knew it needed a tractor to add to its line of farm equipment if it was to remain competitive in the market. Farmers wanted the option of buying all of their equipment at one place and all of the major manufacturers were starting to supply their demands.

Oliver had worked closely for many years with Henry Ford. They supplied the plows and other tillage tools that could be purchased with the very popular Ford tractors. Row crop tractors were becoming more widespread but Henry refused to change with the times: He was more interested in cars. Oliver saw this as an opportunity to fill the void created by Ford and acted on it.

In the mid-1920s, under the engineering leadership of Herman Altgelt, Oliver built its first experimental tractor. This tractor, known to collectors as the "Chilled Plow" tractor, spent several years in experimental phases on farms in Texas and Iowa. It was powered with a Hercules four-cylinder in-line engine. The name "Oliver" was cast into the sides of the radiator. Originally, the tractors were gray with red wheels and red lettering.

Since Oliver was an implement manufacturer, it was important to fit the machine to work with its products. Thus, Herman, assisted by his brother, Rudy, created the pipe-mounted implement systems. Patented by Oliver, this system proved to be very successful and was used for years.

It is believed that 26 Chilled Plow tractors were built and that two of them are known to exist today. The row-crop variation was known

The sleek 70 was the first streamlined tractor to be built by Oliver. It was also the first model to appear without the Hart-Parr name on it. *Edwin H. Gabel*

Built during the production time of the styled 60 and 70, the 80 remained unstyled. The tractor that was to replace the 80 was already on the drawing board, so updating the current model would have been a waste of money, thus it never received the stylish sheet metal of the other models. *Jim Kline*

as the model A and the standard-tread model was known as the model B.

Oliver realized that the cost of tooling up for production of this model was going to be extreme, so prior to its big jump into tractor production, it stepped back and took a second look. By acquiring a company that already had a facility, machines, and a well-established name, it could cut the cost of this new venture as well as eliminate one of its competitors.

At that same time the Hart-Parr Tractor Works was experiencing problems of its own. Charles Hart had left the company and it was now being run by bankers who knew little about the mechanics of a tractor. But, they too, saw the need for a full-line company and knew that somehow they would have to start supplying implements to go with their tractors.

On April 1, 1929, the Hart-Parr Tractor Works, Oliver Chilled Plow Works, and the Nichols & Shepard Company of Battle Creek, Michigan, merged to become the Oliver Farm Equipment Company. Within three months the American Seeding Company of Springfield, Ohio, joined the company.

Oliver dealers were now able to supply the farmer with any piece of equipment he needed. Tractors were built in the Charles City plant; Oliver continued to build the tillage tools in South Bend, Indiana; Battle Creek manufactured the harvesting machinery; and American Seeding manufactured all the planting equipment.

Using the knowledge gained by the testing of the Chilled Plow tractor, the new company went to work to design a new row-crop tractor. Hart-Parr already had a good name as a reputable tractor manufacturer and it had the tooling. It was also working on an experimental Hart-Parr drive train using a Waukesha L-head engine. Using the ideas of both companies, a

The pipe-mounted implement system was first used in production in 1930. This system was innovated by the Oliver Chilled Plow Works when they were experimenting with their "Chilled Plow" tractor in the late 1920s. It was used successfully for many types of work for a quarter of a century.

25

Above: The 28-44 could operate efficiently on gasoline, kerosene, or No.1 distillate. The Ensign carburetor was used into early production of the 90 and 99. In 1938 fuel was supplied through a Schebler carburetor.

Right: Industrial models used a different numbering system from the agricultural models. The 35 was actually the industrial version of the Oliver 80.
Dennis Baker

new tractor was born in February 1930. It was rightfully called the "Row Crop" and proved to be a wake-up call to the rest of the industry. After it was tested at the Nebraska field test in April 1930, it became known as the 18-27. Both the names Oliver and Hart-Parr appeared on the cast-iron radiator shell with the Hart-Parr name appearing larger.

Unlike those used in the previous Hart-Parr tractors, the engine was a four-cylinder, vertical Waukesha engine built especially to Oliver's specifications. It used skeleton steel–type wheels known as "Tiptoe" wheels, another gift of the engineering Altgelt brothers from South Bend. In early production, a wide, single front wheel was

used, but later models were equipped with two narrow, front steel wheels. This tractor continued to use the pipe-mounted implement system.

Soon after the 18-27 was introduced, a standard version was created and became known as the 18-28. Although the engines in these two models were basically the same, the standard-tread version used a different ignition and carburetor that increased the rpm rating, thus the 1 horsepower difference in the ratings on the belt.

That same year, a big brother appeared in the new tractor family. The 28-44 was created to do the heavier jobs such as plowing and powering the thresher. This tractor was even available as a Thresherman's Special. It weighed 10,550

The Red River Special became Oliver equipment following the merger in 1929. This threshing machine was part of a successful line of threshing equipment.

pounds, had solid cast disc wheels and even a chime whistle. This three- to five-plow model had a four-cylinder Waukesha engine with 443-ci displacement. Several other variations of the 28-44 were available. There was a Western Special, a Rice Field Special, a Tip-Toe Rice Field Special, and in 1936 a High Compression Special model was introduced. It was designed to burn only gasoline and although it was still known as a 28-44, tests rated it as a 32-50.

During the Great Depression, Oliver made a move that would change the way that farmers viewed their equipment. The first tractor of any kind that showed styling and design was introduced as model 70 in the fall of 1935. Although the 70 had both companies' names on the radiator, it is commonly referred to by collectors as the Hart-Parr 70. This prevents any confusion with the later 70. The introduction of an all-new tractor sent other tractor manufacturers scrambling to add styling to its models.

This new six-cylinder tractor had a covered engine, a shielded radiator, and a unique radiator cap that resembled two plowshares. It could even be ordered with electric start and lights for evening fieldwork. The 201-ci Continental engine was designed to burn gasoline. At the time, gasoline was 70 octane, thus, the tractor's "70" designation.

A variety of options were available with this new tractor. The "tiptoe" steel wheels were standard equipment but rubber tires, front and rear, could be ordered. Power-lift was also a popular option: pipe-mounted implements had previously been raised by hand, now they could be lifted with power, eliminating the strenuous task. The power takeoff (PTO) was designed to operate corn picker-huskers, small PTO-driven combines, PTO-driven binders, and other powered implements. The compact belt-pulley attachment was easy to mount to the tractor and could handle a 22 x 36-inch (throat size) thresher under normal threshing conditions, a medium-size hammer mill, or any other comparable belt load.

The canvas seat was an attempt at a more comfortable ride. It had drawbacks, though. Weather was hard on the fabric and once the seat had a tear in it, the material quickly deteriorated. It could quickly be fixed with a Beamis bag since they were the same size.

Driver comfort was an important factor in the design of the 70. All operator controls were easily accessed from the seat, similar to an automobile. The spring and hammock seat was an original Oliver design, it was a simple, spring-steel skeleton frame that was adjustable to four different positions. A strong, tightly woven canvas cover created a hammock that would form to any size operator. It was very simple and comfortable and caused less driver fatigue and better overall operation. It was truly a new generation of tractor design.

This tractor proved to be very successful for the company and in 1937 it was restyled again.

This streamlined styling gave the tractor a rounded front end with an aerodynamic appearance. By this time, Charles Hart, one of the original founders of Hart-Parr, had passed away. Although Parr was still involved with Oliver, the Hart-Parr name disappeared off the tractor beginning with the streamlined 70.

The new 70 used the same Continental engine but was revised from a five-gear camshaft-drive-engine to a three-gear engine. The three-gear engine is easily recognized by its smaller timing cover, and the magneto and the governor are both located on the right side of the tractor. By mounting them both on the same side,

two gears were eliminated from the timing gears. The air intake on the five-gear engine protruded from the hood. On the three-gear engine, the air intake was moved to be able to take in air through the grille. In addition, the valve stems were increased in size from 5/16 inch to 3/8 inch.

Electric start was becoming even more popular with 75 percent of the 70s sold in 1938 equipped with that option. Rubber tires were becoming more popular too. With that in mind Oliver designed a new "double neutral" transmission offering six forward speeds. The operator could now achieve a top speed of 13.4 miles per hour with rubber tires, but, if the tractor was ordered with steel wheels, the top two gears were blocked out of the transmission for safety. By 1947 the hammock seat was replaced by a sponge-rubber upholstered seat.

The 70 was available in a multitude of styles. The most common of those was the row-crop model but the standard variation was also very popular. As well as being offered as an industrial machine, the 70 was built for airport use and designated as "Airport 25." The Airport model was painted red with a white grille. It is often hard to distinguish an Industrial 70 from an Airport 25 and the serial number plates sometimes don't specify the model. The true Airport 25s are quite rare and collectible.

The year 1937 also brought about changes for the rest of the tractor line. The 18-27 was upgraded to the 80 and the 28-44 was upgraded to the 90. The High Compression model 28-44 was designated the 99. While these were all new tractors to the line, they did not follow with the stylish sheet metal look of the 70. The radiator

This "Special" was a predecessor to the four-cylinder 99. Fitted with a high-compression head, it was the biggest horse in the Oliver stable in the mid-1930s. *Robert Duncan*

One of the most popular tractor-drawn plows was the Oliver Plowmaster. It can easily be distinguished by its rooster comb lift. *Richard Hollinger*

was still protected with its heavy cast-iron shroud but only the word "Oliver" appeared.

The 80 was available both as a Row Crop model with a narrow- or wide-front end and as a Standard model. The Waukesha-Oliver engine was bored-out to provide more power. The bulk of these tractors were equipped with HC (gasoline) or KD (kerosene distillate) engines. A number of diesel models were built and powered with Buda diesel engines. Less than 150 of these examples were produced.

The next tractors in the series were the 90 and the 99. Both of these were available only as

standard-tread tractors probably due to their size and weight. They retained the look of the 28-44 but had engine side shields. These powerful models were targeted toward the large-acreage farmer. They had good weight distribution for good traction. Originally, these models had a top speed of 4.3 miles per hour with a four-speed transmission. By 1950 a 13.5-mile-per-hour road gear was available to replace the previously slow road gear.

The Oliver 99 was advertised as the most powerful tractor on wheels. Its high-compression four-cylinder engine delivered more power than the 90 and without an increase in weight. The variable-speed governor allowed the operator more control of the fuel consumption of his machine. If the tractor could work easily with the load, the operator could cut the engine rpm with an instant governor adjustment. This would allow the operator to shift to a high gear, enabling the tractor to maintain its rate of travel at a lower engine speed but with an open throttle. This was the most efficient operating position.

The Great Depression divided the farming industry. Many of the large farms had been abandoned and created two distinct markets for the agricultural manufacturer. Farms had either become large-scale operations with lots of land or remained small family farms. In an effort targeted toward the small farmer, Oliver introduced another baby to its tractor family in 1940.

The Oliver 60 was a small version of the already popular 70. It was equipped with a four-cylinder Waukesha-Oliver engine and rated at 13 drawbar horsepower. While this may seem like very little power, this popular tractor could easily keep up with any of the other lightweight tractors available. It filled the needs of small-acreage farmers who couldn't afford a larger, more expensive model, and it made a handy second tractor for the large-acreage farmer.

With driver comfort in mind, Oliver created the "Row-Vue"-designed hood. The hood was tapered from the radiator back to the instrument panel. This permitted the driver to clearly see the rows without bending sideways and stretching his neck.

Advertised as the "biggest little tractor built," the 60 was capable of pulling two 12-inch bottoms through many types of soils. In 1940, this model could be bought for $555.

The suspension on modern tractors can often include sensors, gas-filled shocks, or air bags. In earlier farming days it was simply a coil spring.

The 60 continued to use the pipe-mounted implement system and could be equipped either with rubber tires or tiptoe steel wheels. Optional equipment included the belt pulley, power-lift, PTO, fenders, electric start, and lights. By 1942, this tractor had become so popular it was introduced as a standard-tread model. But because the nation was in the midst of a war, very few models were produced.

All of these tractors were the result of two tractor-building companies joining forces with a common goal. Its success left it firmly planted with the rest of the major farm equipment manufacturers. Some of the ideas introduced with these tractors were used for decades. The Oliver Farm Equipment Company was about to enter its second phase of power.

Chapter Three

The Postwar Oliver Tractor

The steel shortage created by the war left little material for tractor production. The shortage was so great that many parts built at that time were made of brass or aluminum. However, there was still an abundant supply of pencils and paper for the engineers to keep working on new designs.

The Oliver 77 was actually the first in the Fleetline series to appear wearing its new sheet metal. Sleek and colorful, the tractor has been said by many to have revolutionized the look of tractors. *Robert H. Tallman*

Orchard fenders made the Fleetline series look more streamlined. All obstructions such as the steering wheel and exhaust pipe were lowered to prevent damage to the trees in the groves. *Dennis Baker*

The Oliver engineering department was hard at work in preparation for a new world of power.

The new Fleetline series of tractors was on the drawing boards long before the end of the war. These tractors would represent new styling and new mechanical design that would leave an impact on every tractor manufacturer to this day. The tractors were to be redesigned from the ground up. The idea behind the engineering of the 66, 77, and 88 was to build a series of tractors with parts and components that were interchangeable.

The Fleetline series was designed around two basic tractors, called the Row Crop and the Four Wheel Standard. The Row Crop had four versions: dual front wheel, adjustable front end, single front wheel, and the special rice field. The basic Standard tractor offered three versions: the industrial, the orchard, and the rice field.

The first model 88 to be introduced was unveiled to the public in 1947, and wore the same sheet metal as the 60 and 70. Among collectors, this model is known as the old-style 88. It was built as a Row Crop with a wide or

The most obvious difference between the early Fleetlines and the Super series was the side panels. The Supers were not equipped with the louvered side panels that completely enclosed the engine. Heat retention in the engine compartment became a problem, so the panels were eliminated. *Dennis Baker*

This Super 88 Wheatland allowed the farmer to have a powerful tractor while using the efficiency of LP gas to keep costs down. In the western states, propane was abundant because of nearby oil fields. *Larry Elliot*

A lower seat protected the driver from being slapped in the face with a tree branch. The protective cowling also protected the operator's hands while at work. *Dennis Baker*

narrow front, a Standard tread, and an industrial version. Only a very limited number of these were produced.

In June of 1948, Oliver marked the 100th anniversary of production by Nichols & Shepard in Battle Creek, Michigan. The company used this occasion to market their new series of tractors. Over 10,000 billboards scattered throughout the countryside advertised "Oliver Begins its Second Century...with a New Fleet of Quality Tractors."

On June 30, the new fleet made its first public appearance as hundreds of dealers and their families traveled to Michigan to celebrate in the commemorative ceremonies. Dealers got to attend seminars, watch films, and test the entire line of equipment offered at that time. It also marked the first appearance of the Oliver 77 toy tractor. Everyone who attended the promotional luncheon was presented with one of these souvenirs. The toys were so popular that within three months, over 95,000 of these toys had been sold.

A sharp tractor that never went into production was the XO-121. The letter designation identifies it as an Experimental Oliver with a 12:1 compression ratio. *Floyd County Historical Society*

General Motors teamed up with Oliver to put the 371 Detroit in the Super 99. This combination created the most powerful tractor manufactured in its day. It had a sound all its own, creating "music" to an Oliver collector's ears.

The new Fleet-line 88 represented the most modern tractors ever produced. Three engine variations were available. A farmer could get his new tractor powered by gasoline, kerosene distillate, or diesel fuel. The 88's engine had 230 ci but the KD model had a larger bore so that it would match the power of the HC engine. Many of the internal parts were interchangeable in all of the engines.

All three of the models in the new series were equipped with a six-speed transmission with a double neutral. This provided six forward speeds and two reverse speeds using a single shifting lever.

The most outstanding feature in this series was the independent PTO. Previous models were equipped with transmission-driven PTOs. If an implement, such as a pull-type combine, became plugged, the operator would have to stop the tractor, take the transmission out of gear and then release the clutch to clear the machine. Now the PTO could be engaged or disengaged without affecting the motion of the tractor.

The belt pulley and power-lift worked on the same principle as the PTO. The pulley was designed so that it could easily be removed if it interfered with the pipe-mounted implements.

In 1950 Oliver introduced the Hydra-lectric system. This lifting system used a hydraulic pump that mounted to the operator platform. Electric switches mounted on the steering column controlled one or two double-acting cylinders to lift or lower implements. An electromagnet on the shaft of the cylinder was used for the depth setting and was adjustable by the driver from the seat. Occasionally, these units developed problems because of a combination of the elements and electrical switches. Manual levers were added to override the switches when problems arose. Later power-lift units were

Opposite: If the orchard farmer could have a "low-rider" tractor, then the farmer with tall crops should have a special tractor too. The High Crop tractors, such as this Super 77, are highly sought after today. *Dennis Baker*

completely hydraulic and the operator had to get off the tractor to manually set the depth-stop washer.

The model 77 was also equipped with a Waukesha-Oliver six-cylinder engine. While it only had 194 ci, it was rated at the Nebraska test facility with 26 drawbar horsepower and 33-belt horsepower. It also had the six-speed transmission and the same styled sheet metal of the late styled 88.

The little brother in the family was the 66. The smaller machine used a four-cylinder version of the 77 engine. This was a perfect tractor for the small farmer. It had all the features of the larger models such as the independent PTO, belt pulley and power-lift but it was compact, easy to handle, and affordable.

All three of these models were originally available as HC (high compression) or KD (kerosene distillate) engines. In 1949 the diesel engine was introduced for all three of these tractors. By 1956 Oliver was advertising that it was building 43 percent of all the diesel tractors on the market.

Another option that revolutionized farming was the addition of fender lights. A farmer could continue to work after dark in order to cover extra ground. *Richard Hollinger*

The brake system was originally equipped with band brakes. This system was effective in forward motion but didn't work very well in reverse. Oliver remedied this by creating a double-disc brake mechanism. This new system increased the braking power by 50 percent with less effort. The independent brake pedals used an equalizer bar to tie the brakes together. This was first used on the 60 and proved to be so successful that it was used throughout the Fleetline series.

Driver comfort was always a major concern with engineers at Oliver. With this in mind the company introduced the Ride-master seat in 1949. This new feature had two round rubber discs that were used as torsion springs and were adjustable to accommodate the weight of the operator. After time, these bushings crack and corrode; fortunately, there are companies that rebuild these parts for collectors.

The biggest machine available in this Oliver family was introduced in 1952. The 99, which looked similar to the other Fleetlines, was only offered in the Standard wheel-tread configuration. The six-cylinder Waukesha-Oliver motor gave a choice of gas or diesel and 302 ci of power.

Liquid propane (LP) gas was proving to be more economical to farmers in certain areas. This prompted Oliver to provide LP factory-built engines. The first models with factory-installed propane systems were built with the tanks mounted upright. This created visibility problems for the operator, so tanks were fitted to lay horizontal.

Many improvements were made throughout the production life of the Fleetline series.

This tractor appeared to be completely redesigned, but only the front end of the transmission was new. It featured new sheet metal and the engine side curtains were eliminated. The back end, from the transmission to the drawbar, still used the four-speed transmission used in the older 99s. Because of this, the PTO was not independent and it stopped whenever the tractor's clutch was disengaged.

Next page: The Super 44 was Oliver's answer to a small garden tractor. Its high clearance made it quite popular with the tobacco farmer and for cultivation use. Only produced for a few years, it evolved into the 440 before it was discontinued. *Jim Kline*

Early factory LP conversions placed the tank in an upright position. However, when Oliver switched to the Zenith system, the tank was placed in a horizontal position, which limited the visual obstruction for the operator. *Larry Elliot*

The styled 99 was only produced up to 1953 and in very limited numbers. The Fleetline series had already been in use for over five years and engineers were already working on the next series: the Supers!

The Super Series

The original Fleetline series consisted of only three tractors, and the new Super series would eventually consist of six models. Engineers set out to increase the power in the already successful 66, 77, and 88, and add a few more tractors to the lineup.

The styling remained basically the same except the engine side panels were eliminated to provide better airflow to the engine. Quite a bit of heat can build up behind those panels, which isn't a good thing underneath a gas tank. This is also the main reason that so many original tractors are found without side curtains. Many curtains spent their life hanging in the corn crib or were simply discarded.

The Super 66, 77, and 88 were introduced late in 1954. They were advertised as the most powerful row-crop tractors built. Small cosmetic changes were made: an open engine compartment was added and the wheels were painted green. However, in 1957, the company reverted to the color red for the wheels at the request of customers.

The Waukesha-Oliver-designed engines were bored out to increase the power of the Supers. The 66 model went from 129 ci to 144 ci. The 77 was increased from 194 ci to 216, ci while the 88 went from 231 ci to 265 ci. Cubic inches remained the same whether it was a gas or diesel version. By 1956, a factory-installed LP system was available for the Super 77 and Super 88.

The Supers retained the same six-speed transmission that was previously used. The axles were beefed up as were the bull gears. The frames continued to feature side holes for pipe-mounted implements, mounting pads were added to the side of the frame for drive-in implements, and a pad was added on the nose for front-mounted weights.

The newest addition to the Super family was the compact Super 55. This tractor was designed to replace Ford's popular 8N. Oliver needed to add a low-cost utility tractor to their line-up and the 55 was the answer.

The small machine offered more power, weight, and features than any other tractor of comparable size. Rated at a two- to three-plow tractor, it was equipped with an independent PTO and a 3-point hitch. The four-cylinder engine was the same one used in the Super 66 and was available as a gas or diesel version. A new "Tac-Hourmeter" was added on the Super 55. It recorded engine rpm, forward speeds, hours of operation at 1,600 rpm, and belt and PTO speeds.

While the Super 55 was only 4 feet tall, it offered 21 inches of ground clearance. The short 73-inch wheelbase made for easy operation in cramped quarters where larger tractors couldn't go. Because of its small size, the belt pulley was moved to the rear of the tractor and driven directly off the PTO. The pulley could be operated in three different positions, which also allowed it to be reversed.

The tractor was very popular with the allied equipment manufacturers. Companies were quick to provide attachments that would bolt to the Super 55. A farmer could quickly mount a side-mount mower, sprayer, posthole digger, forklift carrier, blade, or nearly any device he wanted. Dozens of attachments were available from dozens of suppliers.

The next tractor in the lineup was even bigger than the others. The Super 99 was available only as a standard-tread tractor but had three different engine options. The tractor resembled the 99 of 1952 but this time the back half of the machine was new. It now had a six-speed transmission capable of a 13.7-mile-per-hour road speed.

The six-cylinder engine was the same one used in the original 99. Available as a gas or diesel, it provided 65 belt horsepower and was rated a four- to five-plow tractor. The price tag on the gas version was $2,888 in 1956, the diesel model sold for about $3,600.

The most powerful tractor in the Super series was the GM diesel-powered 99. The three-cylinder engine was a two-cycle type, which meant every down-stroke of the piston was a power stroke. Since power was produced twice as often per piston as in a four-cycle engine, the three-cylinder was capable of putting out as many power strokes as the six-cylinder

Waukesha-Oliver engine. Thus the 213-ci two-cycle engine could create more power than the 302-ci four-cycle engine.

The 3.71 engine used a supercharger to compress air and force it directly into the cylinders. Because it required so much air, it was equipped with two air filters above the hood. The GM diesel-powered 99 is easily identified by its unique sound, which can be heard for miles if the wind is blowing in the right direction.

This tractor had all the options of the other tractors in the series. The belt pulley was located just to the right of the independent PTO. The six-speed transmission was standard equipment but Oliver offered this machine with a torque converter for an additional cost. Fenders, a 12-volt electrical system, and cast-iron rear wheels were all standard equipment, but the price tag was a little heftier on this model. With big tires this tractor weighed in around 7,400 pounds and booked for nearly $4,900. This was a sizeable dollar increase over the price of the Oliver diesel-powered 99. The GM 99 also had a 17-horsepower increase over the other diesel.

The last tractor to join the Super series was a small, general-purpose tractor. Oliver was already content with its large tractors but there was a void in its utility tractor line. Engineers set out to design a tractor that could easily be used to cultivate a garden with good visibility of the rows ahead. The result was an offset two-plow tractor known as the Super 44.

Advertised as "The Three Beauties," this style of tractor, introduced in 1948, combined the power of an efficient machine with the graceful lines of a modern machine. Eventually this series expanded from three models to six when it became the Super series. *Bobby Quigley & Son*

The 88 was originally introduced in mid-1947 and wore the sheet metal of the Oliver 70. It was upgraded in mid-1948 with the new styled sheet metal. Although the old sheet metal was a temporary look, it was produced as a Row Crop with a narrow front or wide front in Standard and Industrial models. *Bill Meeker*

Introduced in 1957, it had good ground clearance, a three-point hitch and a front rock shaft for mid-mounted implements. The 44 was just the right size for highway mowing, general municipal maintenance such as snow removal, or other odd jobs on the farm. It was powered by a 140-ci four-cylinder Continental engine and weighed only 2,075 pounds. Only 775 of these tractors were built before Oliver began working on its next series of tractors.

The Fleetline family of tractors had now grown from three to six. With less than a 10-horsepower difference, the farmer could buy a tractor precisely suited to fit his needs. Oliver had achieved its goal of building a series of tractors that were efficient, comfortable to operate, and provided interchangeable parts. In addition, the company supplied nearly every implement imagined to work hand in hand with its fine line of tractors.

Chapter Four

The Crawler Tractor Line

If you walked up to the average person on the street today and asked them if they've ever heard of Cletrac, chances are they would say, "Who?" At one time, this pioneer tractor manufacturing company was one of the leading manufacturers of crawler equipment, competing with today's giant—Caterpillar. Perhaps this is what caught the Oliver stockholders' eyes when they acquired the company in 1944.

The OC-3 would nearly fit in the bucket of its big brother, the OC-156. *Landis Zimmerman*

Oliver's little HG was not only a good-looking crawler, it was a star. Here the HG makes an appearance on NBC's *R.F.D. America Show* that was filmed in Chicago. *Sherry Schaefer collection*

Many historical articles associate Rollin H. White, Cletrac's founder, with the White Motor Company that acquired Oliver in 1960, but this is a slight misconception. Rollin's father, Thomas H. White, incorporated the White Sewing Machine Company in 1876. This diverse company produced products such as bicycles, roller skates, phonographs, kerosene lamps, and lathes. In 1901, the company introduced the White Steam Car to the public. By 1906, demand for the car was so great that a separate corporation was called White Motors.

In 1911, Rollin White conceived the idea of a tractor that would work on the average farm. Rollin had the vision to see that a farmer could use an automobile, truck, and small tractor as much as he used the plow, planter, and cultivator. He and Clarence were recognized as authorities in agriculture (they owned and operated a pineapple plantation in Hawaii) and together they worked on the design of a wheel tractor that made an implement that combined a disc plow as part of the tractor. Because it was not practical for close-up work, only one unit was built.

A second attempt was made by Rollin in 1912 to produce a successful tractor. In a building on his farm in Cleveland, the original unit was redesigned to carry the implement projecting from the rear of the tractor based on a cantilever design. Six of these units were built. One of them was sent out to the University of California in Davis for testing. Although it did a better job than any other tractor at that time, Rollin was not satisfied. Tractors in the early years were bulky and heavy. This caused excessive pressure on the soil, which in turn packed it. This was a major concern for White because he still had the development of a small crawler tractor in the back of his mind.

Upon returning to Cleveland, Rollin and his engineers worked out a completely new design for a compact and efficient crawler tractor. This was the smallest crawler to have been built: The track-machine concept was not new, but none had been built for the average farm.

One of the major drawbacks to all crawlers was the use of clutching and declutching for steering. Clutches in the early crawlers were large and cumbersome and required a lot of effort to operate. To remedy this problem Rollin laid out the now-famous controlled-differential steering mechanism. This method of steering was accomplished by transferring uninterrupted power to the opposite track through a set of low-friction planetary gears with a brake controlling each side. White's new design revolutionized the track machine and was used by many large nations in building tanks and transport vehicles.

Capable of going where no other tractor could go, this HG was fitted with 36-inch snowshoes in order to get hay to the cattle during a blizzard in 1949. *Sherry Schaefer collection*

The most powerful crawler in the Oliver lineup was the 126-horsepower OC-18. This crawler was obviously new at the time the photo was taken since there's not a scratch on it. *Sherry Schaefer collection*

In 1916, the Cleveland Motor Plow Company was incorporated by Rollin and work on its first production crawler, the 10-horsepower model R, began. A four-cylinder Buda engine powered this small machine. It was met with instant approval from the farmer, resulting in the sale of a large number of these units that were priced at $1,185.

The following year the company changed its name to the Cleveland Tractor Company and in 1918 adapted the word Cletrac as its trademark. Clarence stayed with his corporation, now known as White Motors, and the two brothers were heads of two separate entities.

In 1917, the R was redesigned to include a Weidley engine. Other changes were made to improve the efficiency and add another 2 horsepower. Overall appearance remained the same but the new crawler was renamed the model H.

Always looking for improvements, White again incorporated further changes to his tractor and the model H evolved into the model W. These changes increased the horsepower to 15.5. It was the success of these early models that launched Cletrac into the competitive agriculture market.

The export market played a large role in the success of the crawler line. The government of India purchased all of the crawlers in this line. All of the machines were fitted with a custom-built canopy and air steering. *Sherry Schaefer collection*

Cletracs are big enough to accomplish heavy-duty tasks, yet they won't pack the soil. To prove this point, Cletrac dealers would bury an egg five inches below the soil and drive the crawler over the area. The egg would remain intact and serve as a testament to Cletrac.
Landis Zimmerman

After the model W had proven itself, White again set out to design another model. This time he went to work to create a general-purpose crawler that was about half the size of the previous models. This 9-horsepower unit was designated the model F. It was extremely flexible and when reduced to its narrowest width, could easily operate between the rows of almost any crop. It was the first time in crawler history that such a machine was built and sold. It can easily be identified by its unique high-sprocket track design. Along with this model, Cletrac developed the first push-type implements. Previous to this design, all implements were pull-type.

In 1925, the model K was added to the line. Although it closely resembled the model W, horsepower had increased to 24.5 and a three-speed transmission was incorporated into the design.

The first three models to be produced were given their designation after Rollin H. White's initials. The F and the K were allegedly the initials of the Cletrac engineer at that time.

In 1926, Cletrac was noted with another first in tractor manufacturing history. The model 30 was introduced using a high-speed six-cylinder engine. Rollin had been a longtime advocate for this type of power and met up with much opposition by his competitors. This model evolved through the years into the 30B and then the 40-30.

During the next few years there was a rapid development of various sizes of crawlers. The largest of these models was the 100. Although it was produced for three years, only about 100 units were built. It was a mammoth machine in its day: producing 100 horsepower and weighing 28,000 pounds, it was too big for most farmers, so production ceased in 1930. Today it is the most sought-after model among Cletrac collectors.

The 80 was designed to replace the oversized 100 model. Although it weighed 22,000 pounds, it was much more affordable. List price in 1932 was $4,975, compared to the $7,500 price tag on the 100. The monetary difference was great and there was only about a 15-horsepower difference between the two machines.

Prior to 1936, several other models were added using a numeric designation. However, Cletrac announced that all new models would now have an alphabetic designation. The model E was the first, it was developed to meet all the farm conditions, from row-crop work to earthmoving.

Basically the same tractor as the HG, the OC-3 was the smallest tractor in the Oliver series of crawlers. The crawler on the left is an earlier version. The later style on the right is equipped with street tracks. *Landis Zimmerman*

Widths varied from the narrow model at 31 inches to 76 inches. These widths measured the tracks from center to center.

In 1937, redesign was once again at work, all current models incorporated the streamlined look to entice the potential buyer. The first redesigned model was the AG. This was followed by the B, C, D, F, and H. In 1937, Cletrac offered 15 different models from 22 to 94 horsepower.

The large size of these streamlined models created a void in the compact crawler line. This resulted in the development of the HG. This unique machine was designed so it could be changed from tracks to wheels. This gave the

dealers the option of selling a crawler tractor or a wheel tractor. The Cletrac wheel-tractor model was designated the G, or the General.

In 1942, the G tractor line was sold off to B.F. Avery & Sons of Louisville, Kentucky. Avery then sold it under the model designation A. The Louisville company then sold the line to Minneapolis-Moline in 1951 and was designated MM BF.

As the country progressed, the need for road building and other industrial work grew. Cletrac's vision was expanding to accommodate the industrial market. The FD was its contribution to field or work and was the largest

The Cletrac 25 was one of the smaller-horsepower crawlers in the Cletrac series from 1932 to 1935. During that time all of the crawlers were painted Buckskin Brown. The industrial orange color entered the scene in 1936.
Landis Zimmerman

machine in its current lineup. Originally, the 26,000-pound machine was powered with a Hercules engine; it was later made available with an optional Cummins turbocharged engine. The later models of the FD put out 120 horsepower and were quite popular for heavy construction work.

The year 1944 brought about many changes for the Cleveland Tractor Company. Rollin's son, W. King White, was now the president of Cletrac. At this time King had no interested heirs to carry on the legacy started by his father. With his health failing he began to look for a way out. He found the answer in the Oliver Farm Equipment Company, it acquired the

Cleveland crawler manufacturer in the fall of 1944. This union now became known as the Oliver Corporation.

At the time, there were a dozen models in production. It was not the goal of Oliver to acquire and manipulate the Cleveland Tractor Company. Cleveland was merely an addition to the already successful farm equipment company. It was a gutsy move though, considering the country was in the midst of World War II.

The HG was already a popular seller, having been in production since 1939. Oliver continued to manufacture this model with various improvements made throughout the years. In 1946, the familiar Cletrac orange was replaced by

Oliver green, making it truly "one of the family." It was only a matter of time before the Cletrac name disappeared too. The streamlined crawlers with the Cletrac name cast into the radiator were soon replaced by "Oliver."

In time, Oliver started to assign its own model designations to the crawler line. The first in this series was OC-3 (this model was actually Cletrac's HG with minor changes being made).

The next crawler to follow in this suit was the OC-18, actually an updated version of Cletrac's FDE. It used the same 126-horsepower engine, but gained about 5 tons over the previous model. It featured air steering and could even be equipped with air brakes. The standard model listed for $21,948 and was the largest, most powerful crawler ever built by Oliver.

Oliver finally made an attempt at producing its own crawler, the first since the union of the two companies. The result was the OC-4. The Oliver Corporation was largely an agricultural company and that is where its main interest was. Retooling or creating an all-new crawler would be costly. The solution was to combine the newly styled Fleetline sheet metal used on its popular

Undoubtedly the most popular model available was the HG in a 68-inch gauge track, which is the widest model produced. *Robert H. Tallman*

tractors with the existing crawler; the OC-4 was merely an improved OC-3 fitted with the Oliver wheel-tractor sheet metal.

The combination was even greater on the OC-6. This union used the power plant of the Oliver 77 tractor and mounted it on a track unit. This was the least costly way for Oliver to produce a crawler. This was a turning point in the engineering of its crawler machine as this unit's design originated from the Charles City tractor plant and not the Cleveland crawler plant.

The OC-12 and the OC-15 were the next two models to join the Oliver Industrial Division, the department of Oliver which handled crawlers and construction equipment. The OC-12 was an updated version of the BD, while the OC-15 was an updated version of the DD. Horsepower ratings had increased considerably due to increased rpm and many other improvements that were made, but the unit was still basically a Cletrac machine.

The OC-9, however, was one step further in pushing Cletrac out of the picture. Advertised as "The first completely

new tractor in years," the Oliver engineers had taken over with their own designs. With this model they introduced the Oliver Trans-O-Matic Drive with an industrial torque converter. Built strictly for heavy-duty use, this feature permitted power shifting on-the-go. It also had the luxury of power steering, which could be operated with levers or foot pedals. This would free up the driver's hand to operate mounted equipment. This "all-new" crawler was powered with a Hercules 198-ci engine that produced 62 horsepower.

So what happened to Cletrac and the Oliver crawler line? In 1960, White Motors acquired the farm equipment division of the Oliver Corporation with an option to buy the full crawler line in two years. Surely, this was White's way of "test driving" the company before they

The OC-96 was a handy, medium-size crawler. It could be purchased with either a bucket or a blade for a variety of applications.
Landis Zimmerman

After 1936, the second, third, and fourth letter in a model number represented a particular model:

D=diesel   L=logger
G=gasoline   R=rubber
H=hillside   N=narrow

For example: BGH=B with gas engine, hillside model.

The model F was on the market from 1920 to 1922. It was originally priced at $845 but was later reduced to $595 in order to compete with the Fordson. *Landis Zimmerman*

The narrow width of the model F was popular for its ability to fit between the rows. *Landis Zimmerman*

While Caterpillar would like to take credit for the high-sprocket design used on its modern crawlers, Cletrac had been using this design since 1922. The machine that used the high sprocket was granted a patent in 1924. *Landis Zimmmerman*

bought it. When the two-year time span was up, White Motors bought the rights to only the OC-4 and the OC-9 and moved the tooling for those models to Charles City. Oliver's crawler line had become outdated. It would take an enormous amount of time and money to re-engineer, retool, and remarket it. White was not in the crawler business and evidently didn't care to be.

What was left behind of the Oliver company became the Cletrac Corporation. This comprised the Cleveland plant, inventory, and an office in Chicago. Cletrac knew it would be costly to once again become competitive in the industrial market. With $41,000,000 in assets, the Cletrac Corporation became nothing more than a piece of paper to trade in the stock market. Eventually, the controlling interest was acquired by an oil company that pieced it out.

During World War II, Cletrac's attention turned to profitable military contracts. When the war was over, its crawler line had fallen

behind the competitors. It took time to catch up; it's debatable whether it ever fully recovered.

Sabotage played a role in Cletrac's lack of dominance in the crawler market too. Popular in California for its ability to float across the soil and work in the vineyards, it was not a healthy place for Cletrac to be because it was the home state of its biggest rival, Caterpillar. Many times a Cletrac demonstration was to be performed at a scheduled time and place, however, the day of the display was usually overshadowed with suspicion because the machine had been tampered with during the night.

The Cletrac user was often met with opposition when trying to hire the services of the local agricultural supply companies. Certain companies refused to provide services to a farm if it had Cletrac equipment, so a farmer was forced to buy another brand if he was to stay in business.

Cletrac's marketing department was not as strong as its competition's. It is said that for

The OC-12 was another midsize crawler popular for agricultural use. Thirty years ago this 53-horsepower model sold for $10,844. *Landis Zimmerman*

every single piece of sales literature Cletrac put out, Caterpillar would put out 10.

When the crawler-tractor company engineers of Cletrac and the wheel-tractor company engineers of Oliver were forced to work together in 1944, tension began to mount. The wheel-tractor engineers had the attitude that it was their company and they would do whatever they wanted with Cletrac. The crawler-tractor engineers of Cletrac had been independent for nearly 30 years, and they didn't like a wheel-tractor company telling them how to build crawlers.

All of these things were contributing factors to the end of a great crawler line. Had

Rollin H. White's ideas been carried out, his company could have ranked right up there with Caterpillar today. His ability to predict future needs in the market and his engineering genius were outstanding. Many of his innovations are still being used on the most sophisticated crawlers. The Cleveland plant had the most modern tools and assembly line in all of industry, a plus which was hardly ever mentioned in the company's advertising.

Gone from farming are the simple and rugged machines built in Cleveland, Ohio. Instead, the company's legacy must live on in the hands of the collectors and in the pages of the history books.

Chapter Five

The Three-Digit Series

In 1958 the Oliver Corporation introduced a new series of tractors to replace the successful Super series, that had been in production since 1954. This series, known as the three-digit tractors, took on a new appearance along with a new color scheme.

Probably the most popular tractor for row-crop work in the three-digit series was the 880. There were numerous variations of this tractor. All dressed up in Meadow Green and Clover White, this diesel tractor was stunning as well as efficient. *Larry Elliot*

Some of these tractors continued to be produced well into the 1970s.

The first tractor to be released in this series was the 550, which replaced the Super 55. The most obvious differences in this model were the changes in the color and the new grille configuration. The former green, yellow, and red color scheme was replaced with two colors: Meadow Green and Clover White. Limiting the series to two colors saved the company money in the paint department. The difference in cost of printing two-color sales literature and advertising was sizeable compared to three-color. The familiar yellow Fleetline grille was replaced with a flat-front Clover White grille with horizontal slots.

When first introduced, this tractor used the same 144-ci engine as the Super 55 but was increased in late 1958 to 155 ci. The compression ratio also was increased, resulting in an additional 5 horsepower. It continued to be available as gas or diesel versions.

The husky little 550 was a very popular, all-purpose utility tractor. Rated as a three-plow machine, it was equipped with a wide variety of features. Regular equipment included the standard double-disc brakes, electric start with a safety switch, fuel gauge, six-speed transmission,

and even a cigar lighter. Optional equipment included power steering, belt pulley, front frame weights, a three-point hitch drawbar, a coolant heater, and a foot accelerator. If the farmer wanted even more modern conveniences he could get a horn, a molded seat cushion, and foot rests.

This was probably the most versatile tractor in the lineup. It was produced in many different variations. The 550 Turf tractor was designed specifically as a mowing tractor for golf courses or other fine yard work. This model was well suited for this application since it had a turning radius of 9 feet.

The industrial version of the 550 was quite popular with road crews. It worked extremely well for mowing roadsides, pulling a box blade,

Above: In 1959, after the introduction of the helical gear transmission, Oliver tractors were painted a pale green. This 880, still in original condition, is a fine example of that hard-to-find model. *Dennis Baker*

Left: A favorite among collectors is the high-clearance model, available in gas, diesel, or LP versions. It was advertised as an extra-high-clearance tractor because the front axle had 36 inches of clearance. *Dennis Baker*

Another variation of the 880 is the Wheatland model. It can easily be identified by the protective panels enclosing the operator's feet. In 1962 this model listed for $4,200. *Larry Elliot*

or even spraying weeds. Many companies were making implements for this machine, including a loader and backhoe attachment.

This setup required a larger hydraulic pump to accommodate the requirements necessary to operate the backhoe. A small unit like this was much easier to maneuver in tight areas where larger equipment couldn't go. A tractor with this configuration would allow a wide variety of jobs to be accomplished with little effort and without the expense of additional equipment.

The 550 Industrial was also available as a forklift. The seat and steering controls were turned around to face the rear of the machine. The mast was mounted where the three-point

was and operated by the hydraulic system of the tractor. In normal use, the tractor would have six forward speeds and two in reverse. But by operating the machine backwards, the operator would only have two forward speeds and six in reverse. Gears were reversed in the transmission that would allow for six forward speeds when driving the unit in a forklift configuration. Early models were equipped with a 12-foot mast having a 2-ton capacity. By the end of production, masts were available with a 21-foot lift.

In 1963, the 550 once again had a face-lift to match the four-digit series tractor being built at that time. The metal horizontal bar grille was replaced with a fiberglass checkerboard-style grille. In addition, the oval-shaped Oliver logo was replaced with the orange-and-black keystone-shaped logo. This tractor remained in production until 1975, making it the longest continuous-production-run tractor built by Oliver.

The next tractor introduced in the three-digit series was the 770. This tractor also took on the Meadow Green and Clover White color scheme along with the horizontal bar grille. The cubic inches of this machine remained unchanged, however, the rpms were increased along with the compression ratio to 7.3:1 on the gas model, resulting in an increase of 5 horsepower. The compression ratio of the diesel unit was now 16:1. The LP version was still available but increased the cost of the tractor by $280.

The 770 continued to use many of the features of the earlier model such as the independent PTO, the rubber torsion seat springs, double-disc brakes, and a choice of hydraulic systems. The instrument panel was redesigned with the new Tac-hourmeter, and another gauge that had several of the indicators grouped into one.

Following in the footsteps of the 550, the 770 was updated in 1964 to take on the appearance of the four-digit tractors in production at the time. The bar grille was replaced by the fiberglass checkerboard grille and the clamshell fenders were replaced with flat-top fenders that had recessed lights. The 770 remained in production until 1967.

The 880 was introduced at the same time as the 770 and was designed to replace the Super 88. The 880 continued to have 265 ci but had an increase in rpm and compression. It was offered as a gas, diesel, or LP model. This model was in production until 1963, when it was replaced by the 1600.

The 770 and 880 shared many of the same features. The newest optional feature available for both of these models was the Power Booster Drive. This would allow up to one-third more

The three-digit series had several axle variations; single front wheel, dual front wheels, Wheatland, adjustable wide front, and the standard front axle, sometimes referred to as a stationary front. *Larry Elliot*

pulling power on the go. The operator could now make adjustments to his speed without having to stop and shift. By pulling the Power Booster Drive lever back, the farmer could slow down just enough to go around the corner or make a turn while holding full engine power.

The Power-Traction Hitch was another new option available for both the 770 and 880. This system was powered by an external hydraulic cylinder and could be used by implements with

The 770 was tested at the Nebraska tests in 1958 with its 216.5-ci Waukesha engine. The maximum drawbar horsepower demonstrated at the test was 42.75, however SAE rated it at 33.79. *Dennis Baker*

When the 770 originally appeared in 1958 it had a horizontal bar grille. However, it was replaced in 1963 with a fiberglass checkerboard or egg crate grille to give it a similar appearance to the other tractors in the Oliver family at this time. *Dennis Baker*

The 990 was an updated version of the earlier Super 99. Although its engine only had a 213-ci displacement, the roaring "Jimmy" put out 77.41 drawbar horsepower when tested at Nebraska. Even though it was a brute and a pleasure to drive, a long day's work on the 990 would often leave the operator with hearing problems. *Pete Markowski*

the Standard was now called the Wheatland. There was an industrial version as well as backhoe attachments for this model. The extra-high-clearance model, or the high-crop, was another version, but only the 770 was offered as an Orchard tractor.

The Super 99 followed the rest of the family by updating but did it in a slightly different manner. There were three different three-digit tractors that sprung from the basic idea of the Super 99. These were the 950, 990, and the 995.

The 950 was basically the same tractor as the Super 99, using the six-cylinder Waukesha-Oliver gas or diesel engine. The sheet metal and colors were changed to match the rest of the three-digit tractors and the horsepower was increased by raising the rpm and the compression ratio. When tested at the Nebraska tests in 1958, it delivered nearly 62 horsepower and the tractor rating increased to a five- to six-plow tractor.

The 990 was the designation given to the tractor that was formerly the Super 99 GM-371-powered machine. This machine weighed in at nearly 8,000 pounds and produced 81 drawbar horsepower when tested in Nebraska. It was available as either an agricultural or industrial tractor. The increased power required a 14-inch clutch as opposed to the 12-inch clutch used by the 950.

either Category I or II pins. It also utilized the weight of the implement to assist with traction. Power steering and power-adjust rear wheels were options that were also available on both of these models.

The 770 and 880 Industrials had an optional transmission feature not available on any other model. The "Reverse-O-Torc" was a shuttle drive that was delivered through a single-stage torque converter. With a simple flip of a lever mounted on the steering column, the tractor could go from forward to reverse without clutching.

Many different variations were offered for both of these models. The Row Crop was available with an adjustable wide front, narrow front, or with a single front wheel. The nonadjustable wide-front version formerly known as

The 440 was Oliver's answer to a small utility tractor. It provided all the options a little tractor could provide: a PTO, a belt pulley, a three-point hitch, hydraulics, a narrow width, and an unobstructed view. This model was built in small production numbers, making it highly collectible today.

As the 990 was being produced, Massey Ferguson was working on the design and production of a large tractor to add to its lineup. Massey contracted with Oliver to build a large tractor until Massey was tooled up to do the job.

Oliver took the frame and drive train of the 990 with the three-cylinder GM engine and added Massey Ferguson sheet metal, decals, and paint. The result of this project was the Massey 98. The serial number plate of this tractor actually reads "Manufactured for Massey Ferguson by the Oliver Corporation."

The 995 was the most versatile and most expensive tractor in the lineup. This machine used the same GM diesel engine as the 990, however, this tractor had a unique feature not available in any other model. It used an Allison torque converter coupled to the six-speed transmission. This would allow the drawbar pull to increase when the tractor's speed decreased. This eliminated the need to downshift, making the tractor much more versatile in a variety of conditions. The torque converter did not give the machine more horsepower, but it did save time that would otherwise be lost shifting. When equipped with all the options, this tractor sold for about $9,500.

Oliver tried to take advantage of the work being done by the soil conservation department building waterways. They offered the 990 or the 995 coupled to a Be-Ge Roto-Haul scraper as the perfect unit for ditching. Despite its usefulness for this purpose, the company didn't sell very many. However, Oliver eventually purchased the Be-Ge company, which was a manufacturer of hydraulic pull-type equipment, located in Gilroy, California.

Many parts of the 900 series were interchangeable, as were many of the options. All

OLIVER 550

FULL 3-PLOW ALL-PURPOSE TRACTOR

The 550, which evolved from the Super 55, has to be the most popular utility tractor offered by Oliver. Produced from 1958 to 1975, it was the longest-running production model ever built by the company. Even with the high production numbers, it is still a very desirable tractor today as a usable model. It is often spotted running an auger, or mowing pastures and roadways.

One year after the three-digit series was introduced, the 660 made its debut. It remained virtually the same in appearance as the Super 66 except for the new color scheme. It continued to use the same engine as the 550 with 155 ci; was

three could be equipped with an independent PTO, power steering, a belt pulley located at the rear of the tractor, and a hydraulic system. The operator's platform was wide and flat, allowing for ample room for the driver and enough room to stand while driving. A large weatherproof cab was even available for an additional fee.

available as a row crop with adjustable wide front, single front, or dual front wheels; was available as a gas or diesel models; and continued to offer the belt pulley on the side of the tractor, the independent PTO, Hydra-lectric or manual hydraulics and a hitch. The pipe-mounted implement system that became an Oliver standard in

Produced from 1959 to 1964, the 660 was the only tractor in the three-digit series to retain the appearance of the earlier Fleetline models even when the four-digit checkerboard grilles were used on the rest of the line. As most models were updated and evolved into a new series, this small row-crop tractor was phased out.

New, Full 3-Plow Oliver 660 Tractor

1930 was still used. Few changes were made on this model, as it was being phased out—it was discontinued in 1964.

The last tractor to be offered in the three-digit line was also the smallest. The Super 44 was finally upgraded to the 440 in 1960, but few changes were made in its appearance. The sheet metal remained the same as the 44 but the colors followed in the tradition of the rest of the tractors in the lineup. It continued to use the same Continental engine that produced 21 horsepower. Sales did not reflect much interest in this model so production numbers were limited. Only 700 models were built in 1960 and 1962.

Many companies that built industrial equipment devoted time specifically to perfecting products and not designing a power source. In other words, a company such as Lull Engineering wanted to perfect its street-sweeper unit, not build an engine to power it. Companies like these would build a machine and then buy "Power-Paks"

The 440 was an updated version of the Super 44. It was only built for two years and production numbers were at 700 units. Powered by a four-cylinder Continental engine, this tractor was popular with the vegetable and tobacco farmers.

The 44 and 440 were equipped with a rock shaft for mid-mounted tools. When separate cylinders were used, the left and right side could be operated independent of each other, permitting full cultivation of point rows. *Richard Hollinger*

to motorize them. Oliver was one of the suppliers to these companies. Oliver's Power Paks were available for the 770 and 880 as well as many of the tractors in the Super series. While Oliver did not build a Tampo rubber-tired roller, it did build the power unit for the Tampo unit.

In 1958, Oliver updated a series of tractors that farmers found familiar and comfortable. It was not a line of tractors that were completely redesigned but was a proven line of equipment that was merely expanded on. There were not many unforeseen problems because these tractors had really been under testing for the last 10 years—by farmers. Who better to try out a product and request changes than those who would be using it on a daily basis?

The series ranged in power from a 21-horsepower machine to a 70-horsepower machine. Price tags ranged from $3,000 to $10,000. Every task, whether agriculture or industrial related, could be accomplished with one of these machines.

Oliver introduced their new line with the phrase "Full Power Ahead In '58." Its new features included Power-Booster Drive, Increase Engine Power, Power-Traction Hitch, Power-Steering, and PowerJuster rear wheels

The entire campaign was based on more power. Unfortunately, this series of tractors would be the last one built exclusively by Oliver. While the next series of tractors would also carry the Oliver name, the company was about to be acquired by a bigger fish in the pond of tractor manufacturers.

The four-cylinder 660 retained the older-styled grille, which had been used since 1948. Produced from 1959 to 1964, there were less than 1,500 units built, making it one of the more scarce models. Although it was never tested at Nebraska, it was advertised as having 14.4 horse per bottom. *Bill Meeker*

Chapter Six

The Four-Digit Series

The Oliver name dates back to 1855 when Oliver bought one-quarter interest in an iron foundry outside of South Bend, Indiana. It continued in business as the Oliver Chilled Plow Works. The Hart-Parr Works began to leave its historical mark on the industry in 1897.

Introduced in 1963, the 1600 was available as a gas, diesel, or LP model. Depending on the options, it weighed anywhere from 6,000 to 7,000 pounds. The gas model produced 51.5 horsepower. *Dennis Baker*

These same models were painted red and sold as Cockshutt tractors in Canada. Parts were interchangeable. Oliver had started supplying Cockshutt with tractors as early as the 1930s; in 1962 they became one as White Motors acquired both companies. *Dennis Baker*

When the two companies merged, the company became the Oliver Farm Equipment Company, then, after the acquisition of Cletrac, it became the Oliver Corporation. Unfortunately, the familiar Oliver name would eventually disappear from tractor production.

The year 1960 marked a decade of great change for the long-standing Oliver company: White Motor Company acquired Oliver as a wholly owned subsidiary. White Motor had been in business for decades as a truck manufacturer but continued to operate separately from its newly acquired venture. A completely new company was about to introduce a new line of tractors. The next line of machines would mark the end of the Oliver name as an equipment manufacturer.

In 1960 John Deere introduced its new six-cylinder 4010 tractor. Oliver responded with an

Industrial versions used a different numbering system during the four-digit series. Although this is actually a 550 power unit, the industrial version is designated a 2-44. This was a simple rating system; 2 stood for two-wheel drive and 44 stood for horsepower.

advertising campaign that boasted "25 Years Of 6-Cylinder Power" which began in 1935 with the 70. It also introduced its newest era of power, the 1800 and the 1900.

The six-plow 1800 was available as a gas, LP, or diesel model. The gas engine had 265 ci, which was 18 ci less than the diesel engine. However, the gas engine proved to be superior in power

and economy with a 2-horsepower advantage over the diesel.

The early 1800 model, built from 1960 to 1962, was known as the 1800A, or the checkerboard model. The decals and the grille plate both had checkerboard designs. This tractor took on a whole new look with a large cast-iron grille. Engineers had designed the tractor so

Next page: The 1550 was the smallest "Oliver-built" row-crop tractor in the 50 series. Fifty years had made revolutionary changes in the backbreaking labor of farming. The modern Meadow Green–colored equipment was now capable of doing work that would formerly have taken scores of horses and men to do. *Dennis Baker*

A truly modern machine was equipped with a three-point hitch, adjustable rear-wheel width, and a comfortable seat. Safety equipment was already being installed in the 1960s and included Slow-Moving-Vehicle (SMV) placard, taillights, and flashers. *Dennis Baker*

that one-third of its weight was on the front end. This was the reason for the heavy grille. It still had the Meadow Green and Clover White paint scheme, but the old Oliver shield was replaced by a black-and-orange keystone shield.

This tractor was also available in several different configurations. The Wheatland and Riceland models used a stationary, arched-front axle and had a fully enclosed platform with splash panels. The Row Crop model was available with dual front wheels or an adjustable front end.

Several modifications were made to this series which differed from models previously produced. The tractor was designed so that the operator would mount it from the left side of the platform instead of from the rear. A new uphol-stered seat and backrests, combined with rubber torsion springs, added extra comfort for the dri-ver. The pipe-mounted implement system, which had been used since 1930, was replaced by mounting blocks in the frame used to attach implements. Flat-top fenders were used that housed two headlights on each side as well as taillights for farming at night.

The other tractor to be introduced in 1962 was the larger of the two. The 1900 was designed to replace the 950, 990, and 995 tractors. Unlike the 1800, this model was only available with the new four-cylinder, two-stroke GM diesel. The 4-53 engine was rated at 2,000 rpm with a com-pression ratio of 16:1 and 212 ci. Weighing in at 11,500 pounds, it produced nearly 83 horse-power when tested at the Nebraska tests in October 1960.

The 1900 shared many of the same traits as the 1800 but was easily recognized by its dual air cleaners. It could also be identified by its unique sound of the two-stroke engine.

The new styling introduced in 1960 set the trend for all Olivers built for the next 15 years. Late in 1962, Oliver presented the 1600 to replace the 880. Although the sheet metal took on the same appearance, the checkerboard decal was replaced with a tapered metal nameplate along the side of the hood.

The Waukesha-powered 1600 was available in gas, LP, or diesel. The first gas series had a 3-1/2x4-inch bore and stroke but was changed in the second series to a 3-5/8-inch bore.

Standard equipment on the Row Crop model consisted of a pan seat, safety starter switch, rear wheel guards, PTO, Hydra-lectric, 3 point-hitch, and manual steering. The Row Crop utility model had a few more standard items such as a tilting-telescoping wheel with power steering and a wide swinging drawbar. For an additional

Operator fatigue was a concern that Oliver tried to eliminate. Power steering and even a tilting steering wheel eased the comfort level of the driver. The gauges were within clear view and all of the controls were easily accessible. *Dennis Baker*

$33, the dealer could order a cushioned seat to replace the hard pan seat. By 1964, the 1600 was offered as a four-wheel drive but the price tag jumped to over $7,000 for the diesel model.

At the same time that the 1600 was making its debut, Oliver was updating its 1800 and 1900 models. Known as the B series, the checkerboard decal also was replaced with the tapered metal

The last model to roll down the assembly line of the Oliver plant sporting the familiar Meadow Green color was the 2255. Aside from the articulating 2655 model, the 2255 was the most powerful tractor ever built by Oliver. Its high-torque power was provided by Caterpillar and produced 140 horsepower. *Gorge Coryn*

nameplate along the side of the hood. Horse-power ratings were increased by 8 to 10 percent. Both tractors were now available as four-wheel drives, which increased drawbar pull from 20 to 40 percent. In 1964, these two models were once again upgraded to a C series. This time, revisions were made to the power steering, the throttle lever was moved to the side of the tractor, and the tilting-telescoping steering column was added. The price tag for a 1900 four-wheel drive, C series with a GM diesel was now more than $10,000.

"New for 1965" were the 50 series tractors. Introduced in 1964, the last three models were the 1650, 1850, and 1950. While the cosmetic appearance remained the same, the horsepower was increased by moving each model's engine up to the next size Waukesha-Oliver engine. The diesel engine in the 1850 was replaced with a 354-ci Perkins and the 1950 continued to use the GM diesel.

It was during this time that the controversy occurred over the horsepower ratings on the Olivers. Tractors leaving the plant did not have the rated power that other manufacturers were claiming for its equipment, making it tough on the sales department. Oliver had always quoted the rating of the actual production tractor while others used the maximum ratings tested at Nebraska. Tractors tested at Nebraska were usu-ally tuned up to offer more horsepower than what a tractor could withstand under normal use. Oliver decided to claim "Certified Horse-power," which meant that every tractor was cer-tified to deliver no less or more than its listed horsepower, when broke in.

The optional Hydra-Power transmission permitted each gear to be downshifted for a total of 12 gear variations. In 1967, the new Hydraul-Shift transmission was introduced for the 1650 and 1850. This allowed the gears to be split to a

OLIVER TRACTOR

Utility 1250

Certified Horsepower / Diesel: 38.5 on the pto / Gasoline: 35 on the pto

The 1250, the equivalent of the Fiat 415, was the first tractor in the Oliver/Fiat series. It was used to replace the Oliver 600 that had been produced by David Brown. This series of tractors lasted for 10 years prior to White dissolving of the Oliver name.

to become a nine-year production-run tractor. The 1550 was designed to be a midsized moderately priced machine but it still had all the options of the bigger models. The Hydra-Power drive provided 12 forward speeds and the PTO was available with a 540- or 1,000-rpm shaft. The hydraulic system and hydraulic hitch provided even more versatility to this handy tractor.

Driver comfort was still a big concern of Oliver engineers. An operator sometimes spent all day on a machine and if he was not physically comfortable, chances are he would not buy another machine with the same features. The Tilt-O-Scope power steering system was an Oliver exclusive. The steering

faster or slower speed for a total of 18 different forward speeds.

In 1965, another model was added to the 50 series family. The 1550, a 53-certified horsepower tractor, was designed to eventually replace the 770. The 770 was produced for a few more years

The twin air cleaners on the 1950 quickly indicate that it's equipped with the dependable GM diesel. Offered in a wide variety of models, Oliver even pointed out that it would take the place of a crawler tractor, making the 1950 the most powerful row-crop tractor on the market.

OLIVER 1950 TRACTOR
105 certified pto horsepower

column would tilt to three positions and allowed the driver to stand up and drive with safety and comfort. The recessed wheel would also telescope 5 inches to accommodate arm length. The deep-cushioned seat was an extra that could be adjusted to fit individual operator weight. A cushioned armrest was available to permit the operator to sit side-saddle in comfort while watching trailing implements. The controls on the dash were all positioned conveniently in reach and the lighted gauges were right within view.

PowerJuster wheels were an option that allowed the operator to make tread adjustments virtually labor free. The rims were fitted with a spiral-type track. By loosening a few bolts, the operator could use the power of the tractor to spin the wheels to different widths from 61 to 98 inches, depending on the wheels. Tightening the bolts back down locked the wheels into this width.

The 50-series family continued to grow with the addition of the 1750 in 1966. Rated at a five-to six-plow tractor, this model continued to use the Waukesha-Oliver engine in both gas and diesel. The engines were the same size as those used in the 1800 B and C, but the rated speed was increased to produce more power. Oliver now offered a lineup of six models ranging from 38.5 to 105 PTO horsepower.

All of these models had the same cosmetic appearance except for one: the 1250 was a small utility tractor that was added to target the small farmer or gardener. It was also produced in a Vineyard and Turf model. Oliver had felt the need to supply a smaller tractor to replace the 550, but the cost of tooling up for a completely new model was not feasible. Instead, it contracted with Fiat of Italy to build it for them. This resulted in a working relationship between the two companies that lasted 10 years.

During that time seven different models were built for Oliver: 1250, 1255, 1265, 1355, 1365, 1450, and 1465. Although they didn't look exactly like their bigger siblings, they were painted Oliver green and a checkerboard type of grille was used to tie it together. These little four-cylinder models were produced in gas and diesel and were all wide-front models. They were even available as four-wheel drives. Although these tractors were not American-made Olivers, they were still a part of the Oliver family.

The family continued to grow with the introduction of the 1950-T in 1967. This was Oliver's first factory turbocharged model and was designed to replace the 1950 with the GM diesel. While this tractor used the same styling and many of the same features as the others, it was the first to use the new Over/Under Hydraul-Shift transmission. This new feature would allow the driver to select the travel speed on-the-go with the flip of a lever mounted on the right side of the dash. Underdrive allowed a 20 percent boost in pulling power while overdrive increased the speed by 20 percent when the load let up. Speeds ranged from 0.6 in creeper gear underdrive to 17.2 in sixth-gear overdrive.

As tractors got larger in size and power, more fuel was necessary. Running back to the farm for more fuel cut into the amount of work that could be done. To remedy this problem, Oliver engineers created the wheel-guard fuel tanks. Each fender was actually a fuel tank with a 39-gallon capacity. This would permit long runs in the field without having to refuel.

The 1950-T was now the biggest tractor in the Oliver lineup. It was meant to go to the field for the big jobs and to stay there. To make the day a little more comfortable for the operator, Oliver offered a roomy cab that was built by Continental. It was designed with visibility on all sides and tinted safety glass. The overhead blower with standard equipment and air conditioning was available, as was a heater, wipers, radio, and stereo-tape player. There was a door on each side of the cab with steps below; the Wheatland tractor cab had a door at the back for a rear exit.

Within a year of the introduction of the 1950-T, two more even larger tractors would become part of the Oliver family. The 2050 and the 2150 were basically the same machines. Both of them shared the 478-ci White-Hercules diesel engine, but the 2150 was turbocharged. Both were available as two-wheel or four-wheel drive models. Options for both machines included the Hydraul-Shift, a cab, and the twin wheel-guard fuel tanks. Fuel capacity with the standard tank and the fender tanks totaled 105 gallons.

The 2150 also was offered as an extra-heavy-duty (EHD) model. This tractor had planetary gear drives on the rear axle as well as on the front. This reduced the axle torque 75 percent to permit a high-speed, low-torque power transfer at the bull gears. Rated at 131 PTO horsepower, the 2150 was now one of the most powerful tractors available from any manufacturer. Both of these models were built until 1969.

Late in 1969, the White Motor Company reorganized as the White Farm Equipment Company. As a result, Oliver was consolidated with Minneapolis-Moline (MM).

The 55 series was introduced after the consolidation of Oliver and Minneapolis-Moline. The most obvious physical difference between the 50 series and the 55 series is the placement of the headlights to the inside of the grille. These tractors were popular with the large-acreage farmer and are still widely used today.

OLIVER TRACTORS

1755/1855/1955

The first tractor of the 55 series was built as a shared model between the two companies also was the largest tractor offered at the time. The 2455 was an articulating model that was built by MM. It was powered by a 504-ci, six-cylinder diesel MM engine. This was the first tractor of this type to be offered by either company and it weighed in at 19,000 with 139 horsepower. The production of this model only lasted two years when it then evolved into the 2655.

Production of the articulating models continued by MM. The 2655 was the Oliver version of the A4T-1600. The engine size was increased to 585 ci and the power jumped to 169 horsepower. This same tractor was produced in three different versions: The first used the familiar Meadow Green paint with Oliver's name on the side and was painted white on the front of the grille. The second variation was simply a MM-colored tractor with the MM logo. The last variation was the

No longer did farm work consist of just pulling an implement. To be versatile, a tractor needed to be equipped with a three-point hitch, PTO, and hydraulics. What were once options, were now necessities.

Continental offered three different cab models for this series of tractor: the Row Crop, Wheatland, and Narrow Row Cab. The cost for a basic cab started at $790. Each option, such as a Motorola radio or Borg-Warner 8-track player, added to the list price. The air conditioner unit added an additional $689, nearly doubling the price of the cab. *Everett Jensen*

General Motors continued to supply Oliver with engines after the introduction of the four-digit series. This 4:53 engine was used in the 1900 and 1950, and produced 105.79 PTO horsepower. *Everett Jensen*

Plainsman. This tractor was painted red, white, and blue in honor of the Heritage series.

Minneapolis-Moline built several other models that they shared with Oliver. The MM G-950 also was sold as the Oliver 1865. The MM G-1050 was sold as the Oliver 2055, and the MM G-1350 was offered as the Oliver 2155.

While all these changes were taking place, the familiar 50 series tractors were upgraded to the 55 series. The 1550 became the 1555, the 1650 became the 1655, and likewise throughout the rest of the model line. The appearance remained the same except for a few minor changes. A striped decal was placed on the fenders and headlights were added to the front grille.

Minneapolis-Moline shared its large models with Oliver, and Oliver shared its mid-size tractors with MM. The Oliver 1555 was sold as the MM G-550, the Oliver 1655 was sold as the G-750, the 1755 as the G-850, and the 1855 as the G-940. Other than the difference in color and numbering, the tractors were identical.

The end was drawing near for a company whose name had appeared on farm equipment for nearly 120 years. The last Oliver tractor to be manufactured at the Charles City, Iowa, plant was the 2255. It looked like the rest of the models in the 55 series, but it was the only Oliver that ever used a V-8 engine. When first introduced, it used a 573-ci 3150 Caterpillar

Equipped with Oliver's Continental cab, this tractor was prepared to spend the day in the field. Each of the fenders had a capacity of 39 gallons of fuel. The SMV emblem became standard equipment in 1966. *Everett Jensen*

engine that produced 146 PTO horsepower, when tested at Nebraska in 1973. Later this engine was replaced by a 636-ci 3208 Caterpillar engine. The 2255 with the larger engine was never tested at Nebraska but was advertised as a 147-PTO tractor.

As the country was celebrating 200 years of freedom, the last Oliver tractor was rolling out the door. The 2255 was the last tractor to be built with the Oliver name and Meadow Green color, ending 75 years of tractor production at the Charles City plant. Oliver had been a name synonymous with the farm equipment industry for 130 years. As AGCO continues to manufacture White equipment, Oliver has been reduced to the history books, leaving the industry with innovations that were ahead of their time.

Index

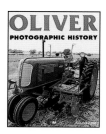
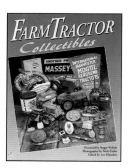

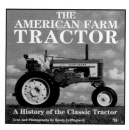

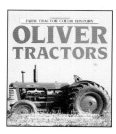